W9-AET-374

IS THE TRUMPET FOR YOU?

ELAINE LANDAU

Lerner Publications Company · Minneapolis

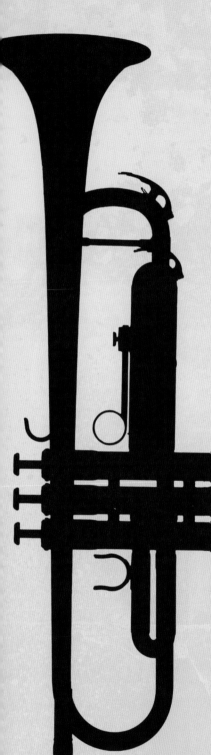

Lerner Publications Company
A division of Lerner Publishing Group, Inc.
241 First Avenue North
Minneapolis, MN 55401 U.S.A.

Website address: www.lernerbooks.com

Library of Congress Cataloging-in-Publication Data

Landau, Elaine.
     Is the trumpet for you? / by Elaine Landau.
        p.   cm. — (Ready to make music)
     Includes bibliographical references and index.
     ISBN 978-0-7613-5422-2 (lib. bdg. : alk. paper)
     1. Trumpet—Juvenile literature. I. Title.
ML960.L36 2011
788.9'2—dc22   2009048280

Manufactured in the United States of America
1 – DP – 7/15/10

C**O**NTENTS

CHAPTER ONE

GREAT GLEAMING BRASS

Picture this:

You're a trumpeter in a symphony orchestra. You're about to play a solo. You're nervous, but you shouldn't be. You play your part perfectly. You know it, and so does the audience. You've done what you set out to do with style and class.

Shift to another scene. You're a trumpeter with a great rock band. Tonight your band is playing many songs that feature your fabulous horn. You blow into your trumpet like never before. For a few minutes, it's just you and your trumpet onstage.

4

Trumpeters can play all kinds of music.

Trumpet player Achilleas Anastasopoulos *(center)* performs with the rock band the Dandy Warhols in 2005.

The crowd feels the pulse of your music. You rock, and they can't get enough of you. Thunderous applause fills the arena.

Can you see yourself as one of these musicians? Well, the trumpet is used to play many types of music. If you master the trumpet, you might be either one someday.

But what about today? Are you thinking about playing the trumpet? It's a great instrument. If you have any doubts, just ask any professional trumpeter. What makes the trumpet so special? Here's just the short list.

TRUMPETS ARE A TERRIFIC SIZE

The trumpet is small enough to take with you on the go. You can carry your instrument on a bus, a train, or a plane. Try doing that with a piano or a tuba. You won't have much luck!

But do you want to know a little secret about the trumpet? Although it's compact, it's really not as small as it looks. The standard trumpet is actually made up of about 6.5 feet (2 meters) of tubing twisted into an oblong shape. If you could stretch out a trumpet, it would be as tall as a tall adult male!

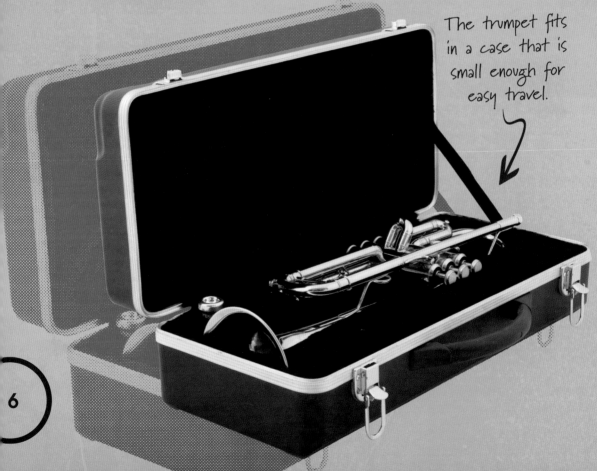

The trumpet fits in a case that is small enough for easy travel.

A BRASSY FAMILY

You're part of a family. You may look or sound like some of your relatives. Maybe you have your mother's laugh or your brother's eyes. (And are those your uncle Fred's dimples?)

Instruments are grouped into families too. The instruments in a family have some things in common. The trumpet is in the brass family. All the brass instruments are made out of long brass pipes that have been twisted into different shapes. The ends of these instruments widen into a bell. Brass instruments are the loudest ones in an orchestra. It's hard to miss them. The best-known members of the brass family are the trumpet, the tuba, the French horn, and th

Trumpeters can perform alone or with a group.

NOT TOO HARD TO KEEP

A fragile instrument is just no fun. You've got to always be careful. But trumpets are durable. They have fewer parts than lots of other instruments. The trumpet is also fairly easy to care for. You can store it in its case in just two pieces. Even young players can learn to take care of their trumpets.

GREAT FOR SOLOISTS AND TEAM PLAYERS

Are you a true individual? Do you like the idea of performing by yourself? Well, it's not uncommon for trumpeters to perform solos. Some even play the trumpet as a solo instrument. The trumpet can be a fantastic fit for people who like doing their own thing.

Whether you like to be in the spotlight or part of a group of musicians, the trumpet could be a good fit for you.

Lots of trumpeters also play with other musicians. If you'd rather share the spotlight with other players, you'll find plenty of chances to do so as a trumpeter. Trumpeters often perform as part of orchestras or bands. Sometimes they play in all-brass groups.

EASY TO LOVE

Who doesn't like the sound of a trumpet? Trumpet music calls out to people. It grabs your attention. When you hear the blast of a trumpet, it makes you feel alive. No one can easily ignore its clear, bright, bold sound.

THE PARTS OF A TRUMPET

Take a good look at a trumpet. At first glance, it may seem pretty simple. It's just a long brass tube with some twists and turns in it, right?

Wrong! There's more to the trumpet than meets the eye. The trumpet has several different parts. Those parts have a lot to do with the instrument's exciting sound. Let's take a closer look.

VALVES AND VALVE TUBE

The three valves on a trumpet are another way for musicians to change the trumpet's sound. The valves look like buttons. When the player pushes down on a valve, air flows through the valve tube. When air flows through the valve tube, the instrument's pitch (high or low sound) changes.

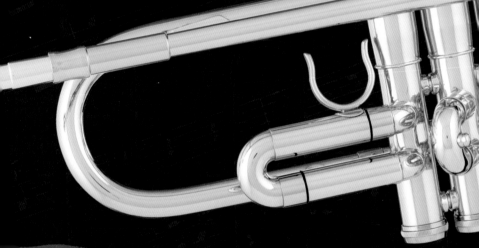

⌐UTHPIECE

⌐mpet's mouthpiece is the small, cup-shaped part of the
ent at the trumpet's narrow end. Brass players position their
inst the mouthpiece in a certain way so that when they blow
their lips, they vibrate (move back and forth quickly). Players
nge the trumpet's pitch by vibrating their lips at different

BELL

The bell is the wide end of the trumpet that flares out. The trumpet's sound comes out of the bell. You might think of the bell as a sort of loudspeaker. It thrusts the sound forward. The size of the bell also affects the trumpet's sound. Trumpets with smaller bells have a sharp sound. Those with bigger bells have a more mellow sound.

WATER KEY

Playing the trumpet can get messy. When you blow into the trumpet, your breath forms small drops of water inside the instrument. Yuck! But here's where the water key comes in. The player presses down on the water key to open a hole in the instrument. This lets the water out. Sometimes musicians call the water key by a less polite name. You may have heard it called the spit valve.

CHAPTER TWO

WHAT A HORN!

Music surrounds us. It's part of all our lives. You may walk down the street with a song in your headphones. Parades have marching bands. Music is even piped into waiting rooms and elevators. And where there's music, you're bound to find trumpets. Just listen, and you'll hear them.

ROCK MUSIC

Maybe you love rock music, but you never thought of playing trumpet in a rock band. Well, lots of rock bands have trumpeters! Just listen to Gloria Estefan's band, the Miami Sound Machine. Trumpets play a vital role in this band's Latin-flavored rock. The brassy

Gloria Estefan (left) and the brass section of the Miami Sound Machine

hit songs by Estefan and her bandmates have made people dance and have inspired other Latino musicians.

The rock group Chicago is also known for its use of trumpets. One of the band's founding members, Lee Loughnane, is the son of a trumpet player. Loughnane grew up with a love of music and began playing trumpet as a child. His playing got better and better. In 1967 he helped found Chicago—a band that mixes bold brass music with the sounds of rock and roll. Chicago has become one of the ten best-selling U.S. rock bands in history. Who says trumpets don't rock?

Blood, Sweat and Tears plays award-winning brassy rock music.

Blood, Sweat and Tears is another rock group famous for featuring the trumpet. This group got its start in 1968 and is still actively touring. Blood, Sweat and Tears has been nominated for ten Grammy Awards and won three. Besides making great music, the group helps many young musicians. Blood, Sweat and Tears awards money to deserving music students for lessons. The group also helps schools buy instruments.

Rock groups from The Beatles and the Rolling Stones to No Doubt and the Red Hot Chili Peppers have used trumpets in their songs too. Do you think you'd like to play the trumpet in a rock band? If so, check out some recordings by rock artists who play trumpets. Listen carefully to their songs. The more you listen, the more you'll learn about their musical style.

LOVE THAT JAZZ

Trumpets are more commonly used in jazz. The trumpet's role in jazz is different from its role in rock or classical music. Jazz is less structured than many types of music. Often the musicians make up parts of the music as they play it. This style is known as improvisation. It allows jazz trumpeters to put whatever they feel at the time into their music.

MEET THE TROMBONE

The trumpet's a wonderful instrument, but what if you're not sure it's for you? Then maybe you'll want to check out the trombone. The trombone's tone is very rich. Its distinctive sound makes it stand out in an orchestra.

Unlike most brass instruments, the trombone doesn't have valves. It has a U-shaped slide to change its pitch instead. The trombone player pulls the slide in and out to do this. You need long arms to work the slide. So very young music students may have to wait until they're bigger to play the trombone.

JAZZ GREATS

Jazz has no shortage of great trumpeters. Wynton Marsalis is among the best. Marsalis got his first trumpet when he was just six. By the time he was seven, he was playing in public. When he was twelve, Marsalis began to study music seriously. Then at fourteen, he debuted with the New Orleans Philharmonic. That was just a taste of things to come.

Marsalis went on to study at the Juilliard School of Music. In 1983 he did something no one had ever done before. Marsalis won Grammy Awards for both jazz and classical music in the same year. Then, in 1997, he became the first jazz musician to ever receive a Pulitzer Prize for music.

Even with his great success, Marsalis never lost touch with young people. He created music

Wynton Marsalis

FROM MEXICO TO YOU

Do you like folk music? Would you be curious to hear folk songs with a Mexican twist? If so, you might become a fan of mariachi music.

Mariachi bands (right) began many years ago in Mexico. Early on, mariachi musicians played only string instruments. But by the 1940s, these bands had also begun using the trumpet. These days, most mariachi bands have two or more trumpeters. Mariachi bands don't just sound great. They look great too. Their outfits include tight-fitting, decorated pants; short jackets; and sombreros (high-crowned straw hats with wide brims).

Mariachi bands remain popular in Mexican American communities. They often play at weddings, holiday parties, and other special events. They are lots of fun to see and hear!

education programs for public radio and television. He's also visited schools across the country. Any young trumpeter can learn a lot from Wynton Marsalis. If jazz is your thing, see what you can pick up from his style.

When listening to jazz trumpeters, don't miss the greats of the past. Louis Armstrong has often been described as the first great jazz trumpet soloist. His skill at trumpet playing and unique singing style set him apart from other musicians of his time.

Louis Armstrong

You should also get to know the jazz music of the big band era. During the mid-1930s and 1940s, trumpeters often played in large jazz ensembles known as big bands. These bands brought in a lively style of jazz called swing. Young people loved to dance to this music. Soon swing music reached the top of the music charts. Trumpeters were an important part of the big band era. No swing band would be complete without them. Want to hear some of the best trumpet playing of that period? Listen to the music of the Duke Ellington Orchestra.

CLASSICAL MUSIC FOR A SYMPHONY ORCHESTRA

Maybe playing jazz trumpet isn't your dream. Is classical music more your style? Trumpeters have a place in symphony orchestras too. Important composers such as Johann Sebastian Bach and Joseph Haydn included trumpets in their work. In modern times, most orchestras have from two to four trumpeters.

MEET THE TUBA

Do you like supersized instruments? Would you like to play one that sounds like a foghorn? If so, the tuba may be for you.

The tuba is the biggest instrument in the brass family. It also has the lowest sound. It's a special instrument, but it's not for everybody. It's heavy to lift, and it takes a lot of breath to play.

Most people would rather listen to the tuba than play it. But you never know. Maybe you'll want to play it when you're big enough to handle a huge horn.

The tuba is a heavy instrument. Tuba players have to be big enough to lift it.

The brass section *(top of photo)* is an important part of an orchestra.

Can you see yourself playing classical trumpet someday? Spend some time listening to this type of music. Trumpeters often have bold, dramatic parts.

CLOSE RELATIVES

There are other instruments like the trumpet. You may have cornets in your school music program. The cornet looks very similar to the trumpet, but some people think the sound of a cornet is not as bold. It works just as well for beginners, though. Could a trumpet look-alike be right for you?

FROM YESTERDAY TO TODAY

The trumpet is not a new instrument. People fashioned shells and animal horns into trumpetlike instruments in ancient times. Through the years, these early instruments changed. About three thousand years ago, people began making metal horns that looked more like modern-day trumpets.

Instruments known as natural trumpets were being used more than four hundred years ago. They did not have valves or slides to change their pitch. Natural trumpets were blown in royal courts to announce kings and queens. They were also used by the military to call soldiers to war. Trumpet valves weren't invented until around 1815.

Trumpets are still important to the music scene. It doesn't really matter what kind of music you like best. There's a place for the trumpet in nearly all types of music.

Natural trumpets were often used at royal courts.

CHAPTER THREE

THE TRUMPET AND YOU

Does this describe you? You've always loved music. You dream of being part of the music scene. For starters, you'd like to learn to play an instrument. You figure that's got to be the first step. You're pretty sure you want to play the trumpet.

But is the trumpet the best choice for you? There's no easy answer to that question. There's no foolproof way to pick an instrument. Different people choose the trumpet for lots of different reasons.

Some people may have a family member who plays the trumpet. They may have grown up hearing trumpet music, and they want to play it themselves. That's how it was for trumpeter Jeffrey L. Miller II.

Kids choose to play the trumpet for many different reasons.

This grandson and grandfather play trumpet together.

"My father played the trumpet," Miller noted. "At first, I wanted to play it because he played it. So he began teaching me himself. I started around my seventh or eighth birthday and never stopped playing. From sixth grade on, I played in school bands. The more I played the trumpet, the more I liked it. Now I'm the one teaching kids to play."

Other kids want to play an instrument because their friends pick it. That's how trumpet player Brian Neal got started. "I went to a great elementary school," he said. "It offered a band program for fairly young students. My friend wanted to play the trumpet. I picked it because he did. But here's the funny part. He gave up on playing the trumpet after only about a month. He wasn't even in the band program anymore. I stuck with it, and playing the trumpet became my life's work."

SPOTLIGHT ON A TRUMPET PLAYER

Vince DiFiore (right) is a trumpet player for the California rock group Cake. Cake is not your everyday rock group. The band's songs are quirky and smart. DiFiore's trumpet adds a bright and spirited feel to Cake's sound. His smooth melodies support the band's style.

When you hear the group's name, what comes to mind? Do you think of chocolate cake? Or perhaps strawberry shortcake? That's not what the group meant by its name. The musicians used the word 'cake' as a verb. Think of it like this: the dirt caked on the window. Nevertheless, people still ask DiFiore what his favorite type of cake is.

At times young people turn to music for fun. They see playing an instrument as an activity to enjoy. The trumpet turned out to be a great outlet for trumpeter Glen Johnson. "I wasn't cut out to play football or other sports," Johnson recalled. "I tried baseball one time. I slid into third base and broke the middle finger on my right hand. Then I got hit in the head with a baseball. This all happened in one night!"

"I wanted to be part of something. Playing the trumpet let me do that. I even played while my broken finger was healing. I was in the marching band at school. It was the right thing for me. I had friends in the band and really liked what I was doing."

Many kids pick an instrument when they enter their school's band program. Sometimes the choices are limited. Not every instrument may be offered.

Students may also not be physically ready to play the instrument they like. You can't play the trombone if your arms aren't long enough to work the slide. Maybe you have your heart set on the tuba. But do you have the lung power to play it yet? You may have to wait until you're in high school for that.

Meanwhile, you may want to play some type of horn. The trumpet looks good. Could it be right for you? Brian Neal had this to say about who might make a good trumpeter. "I don't think there are any rules. The trumpet is small enough for almost anyone to hold. Years ago, it was mostly guys who played it. Today small girls as well as large boys play it. One of the best trumpet players I've heard is a girl in London who plays the instrument beautifully."

How does the trumpet make its sound? Trumpet player Jeff Kievit explained it this way. "Brass players are special. We physically make the sound that comes out of the bell of the horn. We blow air through our closed lips, making them vibrate to create a buzz. That buzz goes into the mouthpiece, through the horn, and comes out the other end as a note. Hopefully, the right one."

"The instrument itself acts to make the sound louder. Pianos make their sound [when a player presses on] a key, which makes a 'hammer' hit the strings. With the saxophone, it's the reed vibrating against the mouthpiece. For string instruments, it's the bow against the strings. With a brass instrument, the musician makes the sound."

So you try the trumpet. Presto! You find that it's even better than you expected. You and the trumpet are perfect together. It's like a burger and fries. True love has blossomed in the brass section. Congratulations on picking a great instrument.

THAT SPECIAL FEELING

Loving the sound and feel of the trumpet is important. If you don't really enjoy playing, you probably won't stick with it. Nobody wants to spend hours working on something they dislike. But if you love what you're doing, the time flies by. Some kids have even missed dinner while playing. They didn't want to stop long enough to eat.

The best trumpet players believe the trumpet is really special. They like the range of the instrument. They love its tone. Trumpeter Donnie Bell described what it was like for him. "I chose the trumpet because of its sound," he said. "I was walking by the band room when I was in grade school and heard a student play a note on the trumpet. I just fell in love with the sound."

WHICH TRUMPET IS BEST FOR YOU?

Think all trumpets are the same? Think again. There are lots of different kinds of trumpets. So which one should you learn on?

Beginning students should start out on the B-flat, or standard trumpet. This is the trumpet most commonly played by students in school bands. It has a wonderful warm tone. It's often used in rock, jazz, and marching-band music.

Wondering how the other trumpets are different? Those instruments are tuned to different keys. They also come in various sizes and lengths. The piccolo trumpet (left) is the smallest trumpet while the bass trumpet is the

CHAPTER FOUR

WHAT DOES IT TAKE TO PLAY THE TRUMPET?

Can you see yourself as a terrific trumpeter? Do you ever wish that one day you'd just wake up and be great? People would pay to hear you play, and you'd wow the crowds. Lots of kids have this dream.

But wishing won't make it so. Only you can make that dream come true. And hard work and lots of practice time are required.

The only way to become a good trumpet player is to practice a lot.

28

PRACTICE MAKES PERFECT

How many hours a day should you practice? People have all sorts of answers to this question. Jeff Kievit believes that you get out of the trumpet as much as you put into it. He offered this guide for trumpet players who hope to become professionals. "Dedicate one hour each and every day, and you'll be OK. Two hours a day, and you'll be pretty good. Three hours a day, and you'll start to find your voice. Four hours a day, and you'll be very good. Four plus (and you'll be) the best of the best."

But what about a young musician who's just starting out on the trumpet? In this case, your practice time might vary. You have to find time to do your homework and any other daily activities.

Practicing at home is important.

What do you need most to play the trumpet? Do you think it's talent or determination? These things are important. But Jeffrey L. Miller II explained what you just can't do without. "Young trumpet players have to have their two front teeth," he said. "The trumpet's mouthpiece rests against these teeth for support." If you don't have your front teeth yet, you'll have to wait awhile before you play the trumpet.

Brian Neal feels that the amount of time you spend practicing isn't always the most important thing. He believes it's more important for new players to focus on playing a little every day than it is to practice for a set amount of time. "When you're practicing the trumpet, you're developing muscles you don't usually use," he explains. "By practicing daily, you're making those muscles stronger. You're also making sure those muscles don't forget (what they've learned during practice time). It's better to practice every day (than to skip a day and practice a lot right before your lesson). Even if you only play for fifteen minutes."

BE A TEAM PLAYER

While practice is important, it's not the only thing you'll need to do if you want to become a great musician. You'll also have to concentrate on working well with others.

Most trumpeters work with other players at some point. Even those who play the trumpet as a solo instrument often start out playing in bands or orchestras. When you're playing with other musicians, keep their needs and feelings in mind. And when you practice together, always try to do your best. Pay close attention to the details in the music.

Many trumpet players start out in a school band program.

Pretend you're playing to a sold-out audience at New York's Carnegie Hall.

Trumpeter Anthony Zator offered this advice. "Whether you are preparing for a concert, performing for an audience, or just practicing at home, the best musicians

Salsa singer Poncho Sanchez *(left)* performs with his band.

LOVE THAT LATIN MUSIC

Are you a trumpeter who loves a Latin beat? Then salsa music may be for you. Salsa has been described as Latin music that rocks. Salsa's hot, spicy rhythm is hard to resist. It almost forces you to get up and move. And here's some good news for trumpeters: salsa bands have great brass sections. So you may want to learn to play the Latin way!

always try for the same results. Listen to the rest of your group. Know where they are going musically. Then together you can create beautiful results."

THE SHOW MUST GO ON

Even if you practice hard and always try your best, things can still go wrong when it comes time to perform. You can have a memory slip. You can accidentally miss a note.

If this happens, don't run off the stage. Just go on with the show. Keep on playing as if nothing happened. Most of the time, you know you've made a mistake, but the audience doesn't.

Other things can happen as well. "Sometimes young trumpeters get nervous," Brian Neal explained. "They forget to take a deep breath before they start playing. They don't fill up with air. Then they blow into their instrument and nothing comes out. It's important to remember to take that deep breath before you start. This can help calm your nerves too."

Trumpet players have to learn to be comfortable performing for an audience.

DRESS FOR SUCCESS

Trumpeter Glen Johnson explained a mishap he experienced when he showed up to play at a beach wedding. "I was told to wear something casual for the job," he recalled. "So I wore a suit rather than

a tux. When I got there, I was the only one dressed that way. Everyone else showed up in bikinis and swimming trunks, including the bride and groom!" But Johnson didn't let it bother him. "I just took off my tie and played my music," he said.

Make sure you know what type of clothes you are expected to wear before you show up.

It's also possible for a musician to have an off day. "Your body is different every day," Jeff Kievit noted. "Sometimes, no matter how much you train, prepare, and strengthen yourself, you still have a bad day."

This is where your practice time will come in handy. Being really ready to perform will help you on a day when you're not quite yourself. Your training takes over without your realizing it. Kievit put it this way. "Being totally prepared is the best way to overcome whatever difficulties you may face."

KEEP THE PROPER FOCUS

Whether or not you have a perfect performance, focus on the music. It's all that really matters. If you give your all to your trumpet and your music, you'll feel good knowing that you've done your very best. And those who hear you will appreciate your passion for the trumpet.

Find out if the trumpet is the right instrument for you!

QUIZ: IS THE TRUMPET RIGHT FOR YOU?

Which of these statements describes you best? Please record your answers on a separate sheet of paper.

1. If at first you don't succeed,
- **A.** You try, try again. You like to finish what you start. People say you're the determined type.
- **B.** You feel that a lack of success means it wasn't meant to be. You prefer to try something else you may be better at.

2. When you hear a good piece of music,
- **A.** You get really into all the sounds. You feel as if you could listen to the piece forever!
- **B.** You think it sounds good, but you don't usually get too absorbed in it. You'd rather spend time working on art or learning new soccer moves than listening closely to music.

3. When you look in the mirror,
- **A.** You see a pearly white smile with all the teeth in place. Your front teeth came in quite a while ago. You'd have no problem resting a trumpet's mouthpiece against them.
- **B.** All you want for Christmas is your two front teeth! You're still missing one or both of these.

4. When you picture yourself playing an instrument in your school band,
- **A.** You imagine yourself playing something small. You think petite can be neat! The tuba is not for you.
- **B.** You imagine yourself playing the bass drum, the cello . . . anything big! You love the sound and feel of a large musical instrument.

5. When you think about practicing your instrument,
- **A.** You get really excited. You think studying an instrument sounds like fun!
- **B.** You like music, but you can think of other things you'd rather do. Giving up free time to practice every day doesn't sound worth it.

Were your answers mostly A's?

If so, the trumpet may just be the right choice for you!

GLOSSARY

bell: the wide end of the trumpet that flares out

ensemble: a group of musicians who perform together

improvisation: making up parts of the music you play while you are playing it

mouthpiece: the small, cup-shaped part at the narrow end of the trumpet

natural trumpet: an early trumpet that did not have valves or slides

pitch: the highness or lowness of a sound

solo: a musical performance in which a performer plays alone

valve: a buttonlike part of a trumpet that is pushed to change the trumpet's pitch

valve tube: the extra length of tube that air flows through when a valve is pressed

water key: a key on a trumpet that opens a hole that lets out any water in the instrument

SOURCE NOTES

23   Jeffrey L Miller II, interview with author, June 9, 2009.

23   Brian Neal, interview with author, July 16, 2009.

24–25   Glen Johnson, telephone conversation with author, July 14, 2009.

25–26   Neal.

26   Jeff Kievit, e-mail message to author, May 28, 2009.

27   Donnie Bell, e-mail message to author, August 8, 2009.

29   Kievit.

30   Miller.

30–31   Neal.

32–33   Anthony Zator, e-mail message to author, July 18, 2009.

33   Neal.

34   Johnson.

34   Kievit.

35   Ibid.

SELECTED BIBLIOGRAPHY

Harnum, Jonathan. *Sound the Trumpet: How to Blow Your Own Horn*. Chicago: Sol Ut Press, 2006.

Humphries, John. *The Early Horn: A Practical Guide*. Cambridge: Cambridge University Press, 2000.

McNeil, John. *The Art of the Jazz Trumpet*. Milwaukee: Hal Leonard Corporation, 1999.

Morales, Ed. *The Latin Beat: The Rhythms and Roots of Latin Music from Bossa Nova to Salsa and Beyond*. Cambridge, MA: Da Capo, 2003.

Pinksterboer, Hugo. *Tipbook—Trumpet and Trombone: The Best Guide to Your Instrument*. Emeryville, CA: Tipbook Company, 2001.

Reynolds, Verne. *The Horn Handbook*. New York: Amadeus Press, 2003.

FOR MORE INFORMATION

Coachman, Frank. *Marching Band*. New York: Rosen Publishing, 2007. This look at marching bands provides interesting information on the history of these bands and the skills needed to be part of one.

Feinstein, Stephen. *Wynton Marsalis*. Berkeley Heights, NJ: Enslow Elementary, 2008. This brief biography introduces musician and composer Wynton Marsalis.

Landau, Elaine. *Is the Violin for You?* Minneapolis: Lerner Publications Company, 2011. If the trumpet isn't right for you, check out the violin. This book covers what the instrument looks like, what music it is used to play, and more.

Nathan, Amy. *Meet the Musicians: From Prodigy (or Not) to Pro*. New York: Henry Holt and Co., 2006. Musicians from the New York Philharmonic describe how they became involved in music and provide practice tips.

New York Philharmonic Kidzone: Trumpets, Bugles, and Flugelhorns
http://www.nyphilkids.org/lab/make_trumpet.html
This site has fun facts about how the trumpet has changed throughout history. You can also learn how to make a trumpet out of household materials.

THE TRUMPETERS WHO HELPED WITH THIS BOOK

This book could not have been written without the help of these trumpeters. All provided great insights into what it is like to love and play their music.

DONNIE BELL

Donnie Bell is a popular trumpet player in the Atlanta, Georgia, area.

DAVID ALAN HAMMAKER

David Alan Hammaker is a freelance trumpeter from Fort Lauderdale, Florida, who plays both as a soloist and with brass/wind ensembles. Hammaker also plays in various community orchestras and bands throughout the year.

GLEN JOHNSON

Glen Johnson is a founding member of Bay Street Brassworks, an award-winning brass ensemble.

ROBERT KEATING

Robert Keating, formerly with the Miami Symphony Orchestra, is head of the music department at Gulliver Academy in Miami, Florida.

JEFF KIEVIT

Jeff Kievit is a trumpeter, arranger, composer, and producer who has performed on Broadway, played on movie soundtracks, and appeared in movies.

JEFFREY L. MILLER II

Jeffrey L. Miller II is a trumpet player and the director of the Coral Gables High School Music Department.

BRIAN NEAL

Brian Neal formerly played principal trumpet for the Miami Symphony Orchestra and the Miami Bach Society Orchestra. He presently plays trumpet with the Dallas Brass ensemble.

DAVID ZASLOFF

David Zasloff is an accomplished songwriter and film composer, as well as an author and comedian.

ANTHONY ZATOR

Anthony Zator, a composer-trumpeter, performs with a wide array of musical groups in the Denver, Colorado, area ranging from classical symphony orchestras to his own modern jazz quartet.

INDEX

PHOTO ACKNOWLEDGMENTS

The images in this book are used with the permission of: © mkm3/Shutterstock Images, pp. 1, 35; © Mike Flippo/Shutterstock Images, p. 3; © Hill Street/Blend Images/Getty Images, pp. 4, 9; © Karl Walter/Getty Images, p. 5; © Raphael Daniaud/Shutterstock Images, p. 6; AP Photo/Gene Blythe, p. 7; © Dorling Kindersley/Getty Images, p. 8; © David Grossman/Alamy, pp. 12-13; AP Photo, p. 13; © Justin Kahn/WireImage/Getty Images, p. 14; © iStockphoto.com/Annett Vauteck, p. 15; Sipa via AP Images, p. 16; © Tim Hawley/Photographer's Choice/Getty Images, p. 17; © Michael Ochs Archives/Getty Images, p. 18; © Comstock Images/Getty Images, p. 19; © Mark Ralston/AFP/Getty Images, p. 20 (top); © Lebedinski Vladislav/Shutterstock Images, p. 20 (bottom); © Snark/Art Resource, NY, p. 21; © Ashley Jouhar/Photographer's Choice/Getty Images, p. 22; © Jupiter Images/Workbook Stock/Getty Images, p. 23; © Justin D. Renney/Getty Images, p. 24; © Bob Daemmrich/The Image Works, p. 25; © Arthur Baensch/Fancy/Photolibrary, p. 27; © Picturenet/Blend Images/Getty Images, p. 28; © Andersen Ross/Stockbyte/Getty Images, p. 29; © Inti St Clair/Blend Images/Getty Images, p. 30; © Syracuse Newspaper/J. Commentucci/The Image Works, p. 31; © SKIP BOLEN/epa/CORBIS, p. 32; © Katrina Brown/Shutterstock Images, p. 33; © Adam Taylor/Digital Vision/Getty Images, p. 34.
Front cover: © Arunas Gabalis/Shutterstock Images (top); © Mike Flippo/Shutterstock Images (bottom).